ALBERTINE GAUR

Writing Materials of the East

THE BRITISH LIBRARY

BRITISH LIBRARY BOOKLETS

It is the aim of this series of booklets to introduce the British Library to the general public by drawing attention to many fascinating aspects of its collections which are of interest to the layman as well as the scholar. Many of the items mentioned and illustrated in the booklets are frequently on exhibition in the British Library's exhibition galleries in the British Museum building in Great Russell Street, London W.C.1.

ACKNOWLEDGEMENTS

Reproduction of subjects not in the British Library are made by courtesy of the Trustees of the British Museum (9a, 13a) and the India Office Library and Records (cover)

NOTE

The Pinyin system has been used for the transcription of Chinese throughout this booklet.

© 1979 The British Library Board
Published by the British Library,
Great Russell Street, London WC1B 3DG
British Library Cataloguing in Publication Data
Gaur, Albertine
   Writing materials of the East.
   1. Writing – Materials and Instruments
   I. Title II. British Library. Reference Division
   681'.6   Z45
   ISBN 0-904654-11-7
Designed by Peter Campbell
Set in Monotype Garamond
Printed in Great Britain
by Oxley Press (Nottingham) Ltd.

Introduction

This booklet is concerned with some of the items of great interest and beauty in the Department of Oriental Manuscripts and Printed Books of the British Library, formerly part of the British Museum. Historically, the collections of this Department date from 1753, when the British Museum was founded. Among the items in the collection of Sir Hans Sloane acquired by the Museum in that year were twenty Tamil palm-leaf manuscripts – then valued as a botanical 'curiosity'. Thus, writing materials of the East featured in the Museum's collection from its inception. Though the Department of Oriental Manuscripts & Printed Books caters primarily for a scholarly clientele, many of its items are also of general interest, some could even correct many a long held prejudice: the first mechanically produced book is, for example, not the Gutenberg Bible but a Chinese translation of a Buddhist work printed in AD 868. Indeed literacy itself – as the present booklet illustrates – the bedrock of our modern technology, came to Europe from the Orient; in the field of human achievement it is often difficult to draw a clear dividing line between East and West.

Examples of most of the materials dealt with here can generally be seen in the British Library's exhibition galleries in the British Museum building.

Writing Materials of the East

The invention of writing, the conscious use of a codified set of signs and symbols to express ideas, thoughts or sounds, was perhaps the single most decisive step in human history. Oral traditions suffice only as long as the amount of knowledge is limited in content and volume. The preservation of sacred texts and traditional versions of historical events, can safely be entrusted to the memory of a specially trained class of priestly caretakers. But creative and dynamic thinking calls for the reliable use of seemingly unconnected data and this need combined with economic and social structures based on co-operative effort, necessitates information being recorded and written down on some kind of material capable of preserving it for the use of future generations.

Nearly all major inventions connected with writing have come to us from the East. True writing developed in Mesopotamia some six thousand years ago and reached the West via the Mediterranean countries. The Roman alphabet as we know it today is a not too distant descendant of an early Semitic prototype. In the same way nearly all processes and materials connected with writing such as printing, the first paper making, vellum, parchment, ink and pen, the art of book binding and various aspects of book illustration originated in the countries of Asia and northern Africa. Why then was one particular writing material favoured at any given time? The reasons are many, the two most important being availability determined by geography and the stage of technological development. Bamboo seemed the obvious answer for China, palm-leaves for India and Southeast Asia, clay bricks for Mesopotamia and papyrus for Egypt while the plant grew abundantly in the Nile Valley. Some materials became a possibility only after a certain cultural stage, involving a capacity for handling and transforming raw materials, had been achieved. To this group belong metals, cotton, linen, vellum, silk, papyrus and finally paper. Tradition has had a modifying influence; parchment was practically never used further east than Iran. In India only the lowest castes would ever touch the skins of dead animals and it was unthinkable to use so 'unclean' a material for the preservation of sacred texts. During the long course of recorded history great human ingenuity has been applied to the problem of providing suitable writing material, producing a variety of widely different yet equally effective solutions.

Certain materials suggested themselves. Stone is a natural, and in most parts of the worls an available material which can be scratched, painted or carved. It has also an element of permanence which makes it eminently suitable for pronouncements relating to the two central institutions of Oriental life: the palace and the temple. Stone inscriptions have been used to record the heroic deeds of conquering kings, the just, and not so just, laws of governors, the codified wisdom of sacred scriptures and, until only a century or so ago, the single deed of a pious widow who perished on her husband's funeral pyre. In Egypt and Mesopotamia stone inscriptions in monumental form, on rough or prepared rock surfaces, on stone slabs, megaliths or buildings date back to the 4th millennium BC. The Persians followed similar traditions and the Arabs whom they influenced also used marble slabs on which to record verses from the Qur'ān or the calligraphic hand of a ruler. Jewish tradition claims that the Ten Commandments were originally engraved in stone. In India some of the earliest written records are to be found on stone pillars erected by Aśoka who, after a series of brutal conquests, adopted Buddhism and was in consequence moved to proclaim his new and more humanitarian laws on specially inscribed pillars distributed over the whole of his empire. Aśoka, who lived in the 3rd century BC, was the first Emperor to rule over a unified India.

The Chinese Emperor Qin Shi Huang Di (Qin dynasty 249–207 BC), who equalled Indian political achievements, showed a similar taste for permanence and saw to it that his feats were recorded on stone tablets in excellent literary style. In addition to commemorative inscriptions the orthodox text of the Confucian canon was engraved on stone 'for eternity', thus keeping it beyond the reach of textual contamination. Only fragments of the original 'stone classics', the first series of nearly fifty tablets engraved between AD 175 and 183 and set up in front of the National Academy at Loyang, survived, but during successive centuries the experiment was repeated, first with the Taoist and later with the Buddhist canon. Carving lengthy scriptures in stone took considerable time and by the middle of the first Christian millennium a method of taking ink rubbings was perfected which produced examples of excellent calligraphic quality and, most important, complete fidelity. A turning point had been reached which was to have far-reaching consequences. Since ink rubbings tended to damage the original which had to be replaced periodically at considerable cost, the original stone characters were soon copied in the negative on wooden blocks. From there it was but a short step to the preparation of similar blocks with positive characters. The result: black characters on white paper which looked exactly like original handwriting. By the 9th century AD the Chinese had mastered the art of block printing, by the 11th century they were experimenting with movable types and from there printing spread, together with Buddhism, to Korea and Japan.

PRECIOUS AND SEMI-PRECIOUS STONES

Precious and semi-precious stones, like agate, cornelian, rock crystal, onyx, lapis lazuli or jade, were mostly reserved for personal use. Even before the invention or true writing, seals were used in Mesopotamia as a kind of signature to legalise contracts or mark property. Seals and signet rings, bearing short inscriptions, the names of owners, legends or figurative motifs were also known in ancient Egypt and in the cities of the Indus Valley (Pakistan) some 5000 years ago. The practice has moreover retained its popularity up to the present day, in the East as well as in the West. A good deal has been written about the superb craftsmanship of Sumerian seals which outshone all contemporary art forms, but less about the still somewhat mysterious seals found in the remains of urban settlements like Harappa and Mohenjodaro (now in Pakistan) dating back to *ca.* 2800 BC. In addition to figurative motifs of an often startling similarity to those depicted on early Sumerian seals, many Indus seals are inscribed with characters in a still undeciphered script. In recent years much research has been done on this subject; some scholars link the Indus cities directly to the present Dravidian population of southern India, thus making the script an indigenous Indian invention, while others favour possible connections with Mesopotamia and Crete. Whatever the truth may be; these seals represent at present the earliest extant written documents from the Indian subcontinent.

TORTOISE SHELL, BONE

In China some of the earliest surviving inscriptions are the 'documents on tortoise shells and animal bones' (*Jia Gu Wen*). This category includes the so-called oracle bones from the Shang period (*ca.* 1766–1122 BC) which were used for divination: a heated bronze poker applied to the back of the bone caused cracks which were interpreted by a diviner, and the interpretation then incised into the bone. While

1 *Bone*
A scapula, incised with the diviner's interpretation of the cracks caused by the application of a heated pocker to the underside. The modern form of the ancient characters is shown on the right side of the page. Shang-period; 1766–1122 BC. (Or. 7694/1554).

貞今杳王
勿琲比
望乘
伐下ㄓ下上帯
若不
我其受又

己未卜亘貞今杳王琲比（堂）
乘伐下ㄓ下上若受我（又）

tortoise shells, being more rare and precious, were used mainly in China and some areas of Southeast Asia which had contact with Chinese writing conventions, animal bones, especially those of larger species like sheep, goats, camels and even horses, served a similar purpose in many parts of Asia and North Africa. The Copts in Egypt as well as some Central Asian people used them; the latter to teach their children the alphabet and rudiments of the Qur'ān. In East Africa shoulder blades of camels are used in this fashion even today. The Arabs considered animal bones, well into the Middle Ages, a cheap and convenient material for writing documents, magical texts or verses of the Qur'ān. According to some traditions, even the last will of the Prophet had originally been taken down in this way. Indeed Muhammad's last will is supposed to have been written on every possible form of material from stone, wood, date leaves, leather, bones to 'the breasts of men' – as Islamic tradition has it. Though there is without doubt some truth in such stories they also serve to stress the universal importance of the Prohpet's message and similar traditions are indeed connected with the tablets of Moses and the last will of the Buddha.

IVORY

Ivory from the tusks of elephants, a rare and rather expensive material, was known in ancient Egypt and in the Biblical Middle East but its use for the production of whole books seems to have been confined to Southeast Asia. Lengthy parts of the Buddhist canon were written on large, thin sheets of ivory by means or raised lacquer letters. The script is usually black but splendid border decorations in gold and red add a touch of luxury. In most cases ivory was allowed to retain its natural pale colour, though occasionally it was stained black and the margins were ornamented with gilding while the characters were enamelled or gilded. Since in the Orient, especially in Southeast Asia and China, custom decreed that the material of a letter should reflect, not just the wealth of the sender, but (more important!) the social position of the person to whom the letter is addressed, ivory sheets were often used in this context. Not only Chinese Emperors and native princes were honoured in this way. The British Library has a memorial presented to Sir Arthur Phayre in 1858, when he was the British Commissioner in Burma, by the citizens of Moulmein, which is written in thick raised gold paint on ivory.

Not so long ago European school children wrote their first exercises, not on paper, but on black wooden boards. Even today individual blackboards, similar to those described by the 11th century Persian traveller Al-Bīrūnī (while visiting India) are an important prerequisite in many Indian, Egyptian, Abyssinian and Yemeni village schools. Not surprisingly wood has always been a rather popular writing material. It was as readily available as stone but its actual use presented fewer technical problems. The earliest surviving example of a wooden writing board comes from Egypt from the time of the Middle Kingdom (2134–1789 BC). In the Middle East wood was used at least from 2900 BC onward until Arab times. Wooden tablets could be fashioned in various shapes and sizes, they could be covered with chalk, mud, brick-dust or wax, lacquered, varn-

2 *Wood*
Chinese calendar from the year 59 BC. Eleven wooden slips (of the original thirty) listing the place of each in the sexagenary cycle. The slips were found, together with many other forms of ancient writing material, by Sir Aurel Stein in Tunhuang at the beginning of the 20th century. (Or. 8211/25-33).

ished or polished or, more often than not, left in their original state. In most cases the text was written with ink by means of a pen or brush but, less frequently, the writing was incised with a sharp instrument. Wooden tablets were widely used in the countries of classical Mediterranean antiquity, in fact the Latin word *codex* referred originally to wooden tablets covered with black wax and bound together in a manner somewhat similar to our modern loose-leaf system. Later, when parchment replaced wood, the term remained and became eventually interchangeable with *liber* (book).

In China some of the earliest extant remains of a wooden book are the fragments of a lexicographical text originally composed in 48–33 BC which consist of small wooden slips with notches at both ends for fastening them together with a cord. Larger wooden boards were sometimes bound into 'books' by crossing a string over each board and then tying them together. Not only in China itself but also along the ancient Silk Road which connected China with the West, wood was, during the early part of the first Christian millennium, commonly used for official documents, records, letters or calendars. Shortly before the first World War, Sir Aurel Stein, one of the last great explorers in the 19th century tradition, discovered large collections of wooden slips and tablets in the Chinese province of Sinkiang, many of them official documents written in a variety of languages and (sometimes extinct) scripts. In the case of letters two tablets facing each other could conveniently be tied together and a clay seal impression could be affixed to a cavity on the outside of one board to preserve the secrecy of the text.

BAMBOO

Another writing material widely used in ancient China was bamboo. There are even theories that the shape of the bamboo cane has decisively influenced the vertical direction of the Chinese script. Wooden slips may in fact only be imitations of earlier bamboo models made necessary when Chinese administration moved to areas where bamboo was less readily available. The perishable nature of bamboo makes such statements difficult to prove though there are indications which point in this direction. The pictogram for 'state archive' or 'register' (*ce*), authenticated at least from the 14th century BC, seems to portray narrow slips of bamboo laced together. At first bamboo was primarily used for administration (e.g. canes, one foot long, served admirably for the preparation of population lists) but its usefulness was later extended to literary, philosophical and other compositions. Smooth rectangular bamboo plates have been found dating back to 281 BC when their use must have been

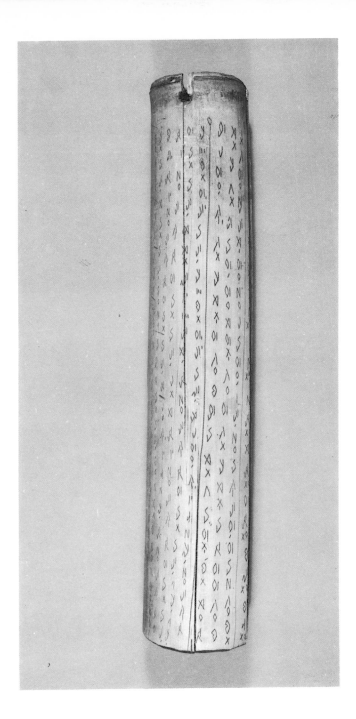

3 *Bamboo*
A 19th-century Batak manuscript from Sumatra. Four pieces of bamboo have been welded together to form a hollow cylinder. The writing, based like most Southeast Asian script on an Indian proto-type, has been incised with a sharp knife and blackened to make the characters more legible. (Or. 5309).

fairly common since the number of books registered in the Annals of the Western Han dynasty (206 BC – AD 25) were counted in 'bundles of bamboo' – not in rolls of silk. Shapes and sizes varied. Small slips, tablets, individual canes sometimes several feet long and canes complete or split into two or more pieces were used or, if the text was exceptionally long, several bamboo canes could be tied together with a silken cord. Bamboo books of this kind were rather heavy and cumbersome and it is said that whenever a scholar went on a journey he needed a whole cart to transport his books.

In Southeast Asia bamboo is still used, mainly on the island of Sumatra among the Redjangs and Bataks, either in the form of small slips with or without rudimentary notches, or rather thick pieces welded together to form a hollow cylinder. Whereas in China the actual writing was mostly done with brush and ink, in Sumatra a sharp knife is used to incise the individual characters.

PALM LEAVES

In India and in the countries of Southeast Asia which came under Indian influence palm leaves have always been the most popular writing material. The Chinese pilgrim Xuan Zang who visited India in the 7th century AD speaks of their widespread use and even mentions a palm-leaf forest in Konkanapura in southern India which is supposed to have surrounded a Buddhist *stupa* (relic mount). Though the place itself has not been found Xuan Zang's report has the ring of truth. Buddhist monasteries were centres of book production and nearby plantations would have ensured an adequate supply of writing material, just as in ancient Egypt papyrus plantations were maintained around Alexandria and other places where papyrus was manufactured.

It is difficult to say when exactly palm leaves were used for the first time. As a material they are precariously fragile and easily destroyed by damp and insects. This is perhaps one of the reasons why some of the oldest surviving examples have been found outside India, in climatically more favourable places like Central Asia (2nd century AD), and even Japan. In South India and Sri Lanka only a few surviving examples have pre-16th century dates. It was indeed only the continuous copying of the ancient texts – a meritorious act for scribe and sponsor – which ensured their survival. Tradition claims that Buddhists and Jains had already committed their scriptures to palm leaves in the 6th century BC and that the Hindu Brahmin priests, though loath to endanger the monopoly of knowledge which alone justified their position at the apex of the caste hierarchy, had to do likewise when the ever increasing number of commentaries

4 *Palm leaves/Wood*

18th-century Sinhalese palm-leaf manuscript from Kandy in Sri Lanka.
Theravada Buddhism does not encourage textual illustration since monks
should not take delight in visual beauty but the wooden covers are the
work of lay craftsmen who use certain sets of illustrations, mostly without
regard for the actual text. The two covers, painted in traditional style,
show key incidents from the *Sivi jātaka* which runs as follows:

'The Bodhisatta was once born as Sivi . . . He ruled well, and daily gave
alms . . . One day the desire came to him to give part of his body to any
who might ask for it. Sakka read his thoughts, and appearing before him
as a blind Brahmin, asked for his eyes. The king agreed to give them, and
sent for his surgeon Sivaka. Amid the protests and lamentations of his
family and his subjects, Sivi had his eyes removed and given to the Brahmin
. . . When the sockets healed Sivi wished to become an ascetic, and went
into the park with one attendant. Sakka's throne grew hot, and appearing
before Sivi, he offered him a boon. The king wished to die, but Sakka
insisted on his choosing something else. He then asked that his sight
might be restored . . . The eyes reappeared . . . Sivi collected all his subjects,
and, resting on a throne in a pavillion, taught them the value of gifts . . .'

The text of the manuscript records the *Brahmāyu sūtra sannaya* and is in no
way related to the illustrations. (Or. 6600. 71).

and sub-commentaries began to outgrow the capacity of human memory. During the first Christian millennium when a kind of cultural colonisation of Southeast Asia took place, the Indian system of writing and, with it, Indian forms of writing material were introduced but, in accordance with local traditions, additional treatment with lacquer, gold and silver soon gave the originally austere palm-leaf a truly splendid and often altogether different appearance.

Three species of palm-trees provided material suitable for writing: the talipat palm (*Corypha umbraculifera*), the palmyra palm (*Borassus flabellifer*) and, especially in Southeast Asia, the lontar palm (*Corypha utan*). Palm leaves are usually broader in the middle, gently tapering off towards the ends. The leaves of the talipat palm are long and broad with a cross vein marking; the palmyra leaf is hardly ever more than one and a half inches wide and shows a pock-marked surface; lontar leaves seem to be of a somewhat finer quality. Unlike wood and bamboo, palm leaves require a simple manufacturing process to render them suitable for writing. Each leaf has to be separated from the central rib, cut to size, and then soaked, boiled (in milk and/or water), dried, usually several times, until it is finally rubbed smooth with a cowrie shell or a stone. The individual folios of one manuscript have to be secured between wooden boards by a cord running through either one or two holes which is then tied round the whole bundle. The boards are usually made of plain wood but in Sri Lanka and Southeast Asia ivory, gold and silver are sometimes used, the decisive factor being the wealth of the person who commissioned the manuscript.

The shape of the palm leaf has influenced other writing materials. For instance copper plate charters (title deeds for the donation of land) were mostly shaped in this way and strung together with a metal ring. When in the 13th century the Muslims began to introduce paper into India, manuscripts retained for a long time the characteristic oblong palm-leaf shape; even the blank space in the text, originally left by the scribe to provide room for the cord, remained, and since it no longer served any practical purpose it became a focal point for minor decorations. It was, however, the texture of the palm leaf which decisively influenced the development of several scripts, not only in India but also in Southeast Asia. All modern Indian scripts are said to have originated from *Brāhmī*, a script already known to us from the pillars of the Emperor Aśoka. *Brāhmī* characters have a rather linear appearance with a wedge on top, left by the stone cutter's tool. This wedge turned eventually into a long horizontal line which in modern Hindi (the national language of India) still connects all the characters of one word; in Sanskrit (the classical language of India) this line could extend to all the words of a sentence. Scripts of this kind presented no problems in northen India where the scribe used pen and ink but in the South a method developed by which the characters were incised with a sharp metal stylus. A long horizontal stroke, following exactly the line of the palm-leaf fibre, would have split the leaf lengthwise and destroyed it. In consequence South Indian scripts began to take on a more rounded shape without interconnecting lines between individual characters. When in the 4th century AD ,writing was introduced to Southeast Asia, mainly from the South Indian Pallava country, this development seems to have continued. To the layman Burmese characters look very much like a never ending chain of circles and semi-circles despite the fact that the material itself (ivory, gold, silver or, nowadays, simply paper) no longer warrants such care.

PIPPALA LEAVES

It has sometimes been suggested that ordinary leaves were perhaps the earliest form of writing material but this theory cannot be proved since untreated leaves are perishable and do not survive for any length of time. But it is interesting that until quite recently pippala leaves (*Ficus religiosa*) were used for painting Hindu and Buddhist saints in India and China. Some 19th century Buddhist works were thus decorated and today Indian tourist shops sell pippala leaves brightly decorated with voluptuous damsels or anaemic looking *saddhus* (holy men) pasted on birthday or other greeting cards.

BARK

Another material which, like palm leaves, needs only a moderate amount of processing is the inner bark of trees. In India two varieties have been used: in the northwest of the sub-continent the Himalayan birch tree (*Betula utilis*) and in the northeast the aloe (*Aquilaria agallocha*). The earliest extant birch bark folios, cut, polished and oiled, are fragments of Buddhist works written at the beginning of the Christian era. There is reason to believe that birch bark was already in use at the time of Alexander's invasion (326 BC) and the shape of some early manuscripts, long and narrow, has provoked speculation about possible connections with Greek papyrus rolls; but the majority of existing birch bark manuscripts copy quite clearly the shape of the palm-leaf. Eventually sheets were folded to create, first two folios with four leaves, and later books in codex form. In Kashmir, a Hindu state with a predominantly Muslim population, that peculiar blend of tolerance and exclusiveness which pervades

5 *Bark*

Kashmiri birch bark manuscript of a ritual text written in Sanskrit, 16th/17th century AD, bound in leather. Birch bark is exceedingly fragile and the individual folios have a tendency to disintegrate. A good deal of highly skilled conservation work will be needed to make this manuscript usable again. (Or. 13300).

6 *Bark/Wood/Bamboo*

A book of invocation and divination as used by the Batak medicine men of Sumatra. The inner bark of trees is fashioned into long strips, then folded accordion-wise; the writing is done with black and red ink. Most *pustahas* (a word derived from the Sanskrit *pustaka* meaning 'book') are protected by wooden covers which are often decorated with carvings in low relief, and secured by a string made of woven or plaited bamboo. In times of tribal warfare the lives of medicine men were sensibly respected by all warring parties and the little note book, acting rather like a badge of office, could at times ensure a safe passage. The present examples dates from the 19th century but the use of *pustahas* has not become completely extinct in Sumatra. (Add. 19379).

everything Indian went to quite unprecedented lengths when Sanskrit texts written on birch bark were very occasionally bound between leather covers. The sheets of some Assamese manuscripts were sometimes reinforced with thin layers of wood to make them more durable, a process which considerably altered their physical appearance and often made them look like wooden boards. An interesting variation in bark manuscripts can still be found on the island of Sumatra. Long sheets of bark are folded like an accordion into

7 *Different methods of writing on palm leaf:*
(a) Ink:
Aṣṭasāhasrikā prajñāpāramitā sūtra, the Perfection of Wisdom in 8000 Sections, one of the earliest texts of the Madhyamaka School of Mahāyāna Buddhism. Sanskrit; from Bihar *ca.* AD 970 (Or. 6902 f.20).
(b) *Stylus*
Episode from the *Bhāgavata purāṇa:* Sanskrit text written in Oriya script; 17th century AD. (Or. 11689;f. 1a).
(c) *Paint*
First chapter of the *Kammavācā,* Buddhist text of monastic rules; Pali written in Burmese on gilded palm-leaf. 19th century AD (Add. 15290 f. 2a).

8 *Palm leaf shape in different materials*:

(a) *Cotton*

First chapter of the *Kammavācā,* Pali written in square Burmese characters; 19th century AD. Cotton cloth has been cut into palm-leaf shape, stiffened with black lacquer; the characters have been inlaid with mother-of-pearl. (Add. 23939 f. 2a).

(b) *Copper*

Grant written in Sanskrit (in *Grantham* characters) and Tamil (*Vatteruttu* characters) referring to the gift of a village called Velvikudi. Tamilnadu (India) AD 769/70. (Ind. Ch. 4).

(c) *Paper*

Kalpasūtra; Prakit text summarising the lives of the founders of the Jain religion. The red dots mark the place where in the case of palm leaves a hole would have been made for the string which secured the manuscript. Gujarat or Rajasthan, AD 1445/6. (Or. 13700 f. 32a).

9 *Folding books indicative of trade relations:*
(a) Thailand
19th century astrological text with illustrations. The figures shown are a
guide to the prospects for happiness in marriage, based on the months of
birth of any given couple. (Or. 4830 ff. 26/28).
(b) India
An account book used by merchants in Mysore. Pieces of clothes have
been stiffened, blackened and folded accordion-wise. 19th century AD.
(Or. 13343).

squares and protected on either side by a wooden cover. These *pustahas*, as they are locally called, are in fact the private notebooks of the Batak medicine men; each one contains the sum total of personal knowledge gained during a long period of apprenticeship.

CLAY

Though India and Southeast Asia have shown remarkable ingenuity as far as sheer variety is concerned, it was Western Asia which manufactured the first reliable form of writing material, namely clay tablets. Early extant examples inscribed with pictographic signs, date back to the 4th millennium BC. The signs were written in the wet clay with a reed pen and the tablets then dried in the sun or, if the text was sufficiently important, baked in a kiln. Once again the texture of the material influenced the development of the script: it is rather difficult to draw circles, curves and fine lines on wet clay and in consequence the pictographic signs changed to wedge shaped strokes arranged at different angles. This new script, called cuneiform, became the vehicle of a vast literature, embracing a great variety of subjects from administration to *belles lettres*. It served, with great efficiency, the successive empires of the Sumerians, Babylonians and Assyrians until the 7th century BC when it was gradually replaced by the much simpler Aramaic alphabet. As the cuneiform script lost its importance papyrus and leather began to supersede clay.

Clay tablet books could vary in shape and size, among the most popular formats being the many-sided cylinder and the oblong brick with convex sides. Because of their importance in relation to the life of city dwellers they were carefully kept in special libraries attached to palaces and temples: they were foliated, indexed, cross-indexed, and arranged on shelves in convenient order. Letters were often protected by baked clay envelopes which safeguarded the confidential nature of the contents. Whereas writing remained a somewhat esoteric art in Egypt, India and China, where its knowledge bestowed definite privileges, it was encouraged in Mesopotamia and all parents were urged to send their children, both boys and girls, to special writing schools attached to temples. This tradition survived and still plays an important part in Jewish life. In the Indus valley, where in the 3rd millennium BC a similar culture flourished more or less simultaneously, bricks were used for the construction of houses (just as in Mesopotamia), clay was used for the impression of seals but, rather surprisingly, apparently not for writing. In fact the only proper clay tablet so far found further east was discovered in Malaysia in 1930 at the site of the ancient city of Kedah. It is inscribed, on three sides, with characters in the Indian Pallava script of the 6th century AD.

OSTRACA

The gradual advance of technology introduced a tentative recycling of resources. Objects which no longer served their original purpose, like pieces of broken pottery, were utilised as cheap writing material for casual notes and other non-confidential communications. Thousands of such ostraca (inscribed potsherds) have been excavated in Western Asia, in places like the city of Lachish, where they date from the 6th century BC and show Hebrew inscriptions in blackish ink. Ostraca were a cheap substitute for leather and the rather expensive papyrus required for official documents which had to be 'tied and sealed'. Apart from Mesopotamia and Palestine they were commonly used in ancient Egypt (later also by Copts and Arabs), Greece and Rome. In fact the word 'ostracism' derives from a practice originally designed to safeguard the constitution of ancient Athens. Whenever a number of people grew too powerful for the welfare of the democracy, representatives of the *Boulê* (advisory council) arranged a secret meeting at which each one wrote the name of the most probable suspect on an ostracon which was then placed in an urn. A certain number of votes condemned the suspect to be 'ostracised', that is banished from Athens for a period of ten years.

UTENSILS AND OBJECTS OF DAILY USE

While ostraca were a well established form of writing material ordinary utensils or objects of daily use could serve a similar purpose, though in a more incidental fashion. Glass vessels, especially lamps hung in mosques were sometimes inscribed with verses from the Qur'ān; as were bridal chairs, couches, wooden room panels, doors, tables (made of brass or wood), musical intsruments, the backs of mirrors, fly whisks, fans and weapons. Leather boots could be decorated in a similar way, and 7th/8th century AD Manichaean magical tests were written inside earthenware bowls. A rather special case are the iron keys from Spain with teeth fashioned in the form of Arabic letters. The earliest and most interesting examples come again from China: bronze utensils from the Zhou period (*ca.* 1137–250 BC) which bear dedications or records of merit.

The sometimes complementary way in which stone and metal have been used for similar purposes may initially come as a surprise: it takes a much higher degree of technological knowledge to cast metal, and thus create a material, than to use stone, a material which

10 *Material from the Middle East:*

(a) *Clay*

Kassite-Babylonian dictionary, written in two columns in cuneiform script, on clay tablet; Babylon, 7th century BC. (British Museum, Department of Western Asiatic Antiquities, 93005).

(b) *Leather*

Leather Megillah scroll (Book of Ecclesiastes) written in Hebrew in a Yemeni hand; 15th/16th century AD. (Or. 4222).

already exists. Yet it is the inherent quality of permanence which distinguished them both and which makes them ideally suitable for the preservation of important documents and sacred scriptures.

METALS

Althought the Roman laws are supposed to have been kept in the Capitol inscribed in bronze, inscriptions on metal flourished mainly in India and parts of Southeast Asia. The earliest inscribed copper plate comes from the Indus valley (*ca.* 2800 BC) but since we cannot read the script we are ignorant of its exact purpose. In historical times it was common practice for Indian kings, subordinate rulers, or persons of exceptional wealth and standing to make grants of land and have the gift recorded on copper-plate charters which served the recipients as title deeds. Since the text of the actual grant is usually preceded by genealogical and personal accounts concerning the donor, copper plates are important historical documents. The plates were fashioned with hammer and brazier, the engraving was done from a draft (on birch bark, cotton or palm leaf), or the text was written directly on to the surface of the plate for the engraver to follow. Some plates were oblong or square, either single, or meant to fit into each other for the protection of the scripts, but in most cases they followed the already familiar shape of the palm leaf and were strung together by a ring which bore the donor's seal. Old plates would sometimes be re-used by hammering out the original inscription; forgers could thus replace the name of the rightful beneficiary. Normally owners would take great care to preserve their plates and if the grant was made to a religious institution the text was, as an additional precaution, often copied on the temple wall. A good example is the great temple of Tanjore south of Madras which had the lower parts of its walls covered by inscriptions dating from various periods and using a variety of different scripts. Not all surviving copper plates are documents. Jain, Buddhist and Hindu scriptures have been immortalised in this fashion. Brass was used, too, though less frequently.

Lead, being rather a soft metal, was fairly popular throughout the ancient world. It can easily be beaten into thin sheets, inscribed and then rolled up for storage. Pliny and Pausanias both make references to lead sheets used for writing. Lead was also used by the Hittites, and the Mandaeans, a gnostic sect speaking an Aramaic dialect, used inscribed lead amulets from about the 6th century AD. Tin was sometimes used in Malaysia but it seems mainly as a substitute for silver. Iron presents technological difficulties as it has to be soft enough for engraving and also rustproof to survive. The famous Iron Pillar of Delhi with an inscription dating from the 4th century AD is a notable exception whose uniqueness for the place and period has provoked a good deal of speculation. Reference has already been made to inscribed weapons. Steel swords from India and from the Islamic world are frequently inscribed with the names of their owners, verses from the Qur'ān or appropriate passages from literature.

This leaves the precious metals, gold and silver, which were repeatedly used in many ancient civilizations. Their use was determined usually by a desire to stress the value of a religious text, to gain special merit by commissioning so expensive a 'book', to show proper respect for the position of the person to whom a letter or message was addressed, or simply to draw attention to one's own wealth and standing. Some of the most interesting examples are perhaps two beaten gold sheets from Burma (5th/6th century AD) inscribed with a famous Pali verse. They were found in 1896 inside a brick, no doubt the foundation stone of a Buddhist structure. In Sri Lanka the entire Buddhist canon was, according to tradition, written on gold plates in 88 BC and, as late as the 19th century, Southeast Asian princes would at times still have their letters written on thin sheets of pure gold.

SKIN, LEATHER

Some materials seem to indicate technological development, as they appear and reappear in improved form at various times. The use of animal skins for writing goes back to antiquity, though it is difficult to arrive at any definite date. Without curing (smoking) and processing (manipulation with oil) skin decays quickly, but once so treated it is durable, flexible and attractive in appearance. By a process of tanning, which renders it nonputrescent and impervious to water through a tanning agent (probably acacia-pods in Egypt but usually oak-bark in Europe), skin can be transformed into leather. As a rule only one side is suitable for writing, hence the characteristic scroll format of leather manuscripts. The earliest surviving examples are documents from ancient Egypt (*ca.* 2500 BC) but leather was equally popular in Western Asia, Persia, Iraq and later Turkestan. There are however certain drawbacks to it: badly tanned leather has an exceedingly unpleasant smell. Al-Baladhūrī reports how the Sasanian king, Khusrau Parves, irritated by this disagreeable aspect, ordered that the annual tax rolls sent to his office should in future be coloured yellow with saffron and sprinkled with rose water. The Persians made other improvements. In Kufa, dates were at one time used for tanning, instead of lime, which resulted in a much softer material. Leather plays an important part in the Jewish ritual; according to the Talmud, the Book of Law must at all times be written on skin and even today all synagogues have their leather or parchment Torah scrolls. The most famous leather documents are without doubt the Dead Sea Scrolls found by accident in the Judean desert some thirty years ago; but other early Christian documents too were preserved in the dry climate of Egypt and Palestine. Normally sheep, cattle and goat skins were used but there are occasional references to gazelles, antelopes, stags and even ostriches.

PARCHMENT, VELLUM

Despite its many advantages leather was inferior to papyrus and since both materials were used in roughly the same geographical area attempts at improving leather led to the invention of parchment. The credit for this goes traditionally to Eumenes II of Pergamum in Asia Minor (197–158 BC) who, according to Pliny the Elder, invented it when King Ptolomey of Egypt, resenting Eumenes' growing reputation as a rival book collector, held up a cargo of papyrus. Though parchment does indeed take its name from the city of Pergamum (Greek: *pergamēnē*, Latin: *pergamena*, French: *parchemin*, German: *Pergament*) it is more likely the result of gradual development. The manufacturing process is already fairly complex: the whole skin has to be treated with lime, dehaired and defleshed, stretched, scraped on both sides and treated with hot water, scraped again and rubbed with pumice, and then dried. Stretching is important; the thinner the parchment, the finer its quality. Recto and verso are easily recognisable: the inner (flesh) part is tougher, more yellow and in general better able to retain ink; the grain of the outer (hair) part is smoother and easier to write on but has a tendency to make certain types of ink flake. Fragments of parchment survive from the 2nd century BC but it was not before the 2nd century AD that it began to rival papyrus in the Roman world and two more centuries passed before it was used for the best books. More or less simultaneously the codex form began to replace the old scroll format as there was no longer any need to write on one side only. Colouring was rare but effective: saffron was used for·yellow (as in the case of leather though no longer for the same reason), the Byzantine emperors favoured purple and the Muslims used lapis lazuli for some of their best Qur'āns. In Europe parchment remained the normal writing material until the late Middle Ages when it was eventually supplanted by paper. The modern manufacturing process is essentially the same, apart from the practice of splitting the skin. The highest quality achievement in this field is uterine vellum made from the skins of aborted calves.

26

Three types of material, originally meant for clothing, also became
established forms of writing material: silk, cotton and linen. Moreover without their use in this field paper might never have been
invented. Chinese records simply state that silk was 'known since
antiquity'. Its commercial importance can be traced back to the time
of Huang Di (the Yellow Emperor) 2640 BC, whose Empress,
the Lady Xi ling, took a personal interest in sericulture. For many
centuries silk was one of the most highly priced Chinese export
articles, its production a closely guarded secret and death by torture
the punishment for informers. There are various stories about
the way the Chinese eventually lost their monopoly. For example,
in 140 BC a Chinese princess who was sent in marriage to Khotan
hid some mulberry seeds and a few silk worms in her headdress;
in AD 300 the Koreans brought four Chinese girls who under-
stood silk production to Japan; and in AD 550 the Byzantine
Emperor Justinian persuaded two Persian monks who had lived in
China to smuggle silkworms to Constantinople in the hollow of their
bamboo canes. As writing material, silk is mentioned by a number of
early 4th–5th century BC writers in a fashion which implies quite
frequent use. By the time of the Eastern Han (AD 25–220) silk was
widely used for letters, literary composition and official documents.
Yet even in China silk was already excessively expensive and in
consequence a method was developed by which old silk rags were
pulped and the resulting mixture thinly spread on a frame to pro-
duce what could perhaps be called 'silk paper'.

If silk was the product of Chinese inventiveness, the first use of
cotton is certainly Indian. Cotton yarn has been found in the ruins
of Mohenjodaro (*ca.* 2800 BC) and there are references in classical
Indian literature to the use of cotton. Mostly, cotton was treated
with a paste made of wheat or rice powder, dried and then rubbed
smooth with a cowrie shell or a stone. The result was a firm yet
flexible material well suited for writing letters, drafts of documents
and also whole manuscripts. Even today the travelling astologers
of Rajasthan carry cotton scrolls inscribed with charts, horoscopes
and multicoloured texts which they take pains to explain to their
village audiences. Sometimes cotton was treated so ingeniously that
it created the impression of an entirely different material. In South
India the merchant communities in the Mysore area used, until
fairly recent times, special account books called *Kaditam*. Long sheets
of cotton were seasoned and stiffened with a paste made of tamarind
seeds, blackened with charcoal (which gave them the appearance
of crude Southeast Asian paper), folded like an accordion and the
writing was then done with chalk or a steatite pencil. Since folding

books are practically unknown in India it is perhaps not unreasonable to assume that the Mysore traders, who had connections with the East, had originally copied a foreign prototype. In Burma pieces of cotton cloth could be cut into palm-leaf shape and stiffened with black lacquer, a slow and painstaking process (successive coats, each one requiring a fairly long drying interval, have to be applied on top of each other) during which the letters were inlaid with mother-of-pearl. The result was stiff black boards, which do not even remotely resemble cotton, and manuscripts of this kind have in the past often been wrongly classified.

The third clothing material, linen, was used in dynastic Egypt as a writing material; mummy wrappings dating from the 6th dynasty have been found inscribed with passages from the Book of the Dead. Later, linen was used by the Copts and Arabs, and Livy (59 BC–AD17) speaks of the *libri lintei* (linen books) which were used in Rome during his time. For writing black or gold ink was used but in some cases the text was embroidered or woven into the fabric. In Islamic times articles of clothing could sometimes take the place of writing material; turbans were inscribed with the whole text of the Qu'rān, linen shirts with marriage contracts.

PAPYRUS, PAPER, RICE-PAPER

There remain two more types of writing material, both familiar, both requiring rather complex manufacturing processes: papyrus and paper. For almost four thousand years papyrus dominated the cultural life, first of Egypt, later of the Mediterranean world, and at times even of the Middle East and Europe. Though other materials were simultaneously in use none was as serviceable and as pleasing and none could be produced as readily in equal quantities. It is generally thought that papyrus was first used by Egyptian priests. Some of the earliest surviving examples date from 3300 BC. The production itself was at all times a highly profitable state monopoly, first of Egypt

11 *Paper*

(a) Chinese translation (*Jingang banruoboluomi jing*) of the *Diamond Sutra,* a Buddhist work originally composed in Sanskrit (*Vajracchedikā prajñāpāramitā sūtra*). The scroll, dated AD 868, is generally considered the oldest (complete and dated) printed book in existence. (Or. 8210 P.2.).

(b) Some of the earliest surviving examples of block print are the 'one million Buddhist charms' printed by order of the pious Japanese Empress Shōtoku between AD 762 and 769. They were placed in small wooded pagodas and distributed to Buddhist temples throughout Japan. (Or 60.d.1).

凡欲讀經先念淨口業真言
唵 脩唎 脩唎 摩訶脩唎 脩脩唎 薩婆訶
奉請青除災金剛
奉請辟毒金剛 奉請黃隨求金剛
奉請白淨水金剛 奉請赤聲金剛
奉請紫賢金剛 奉請定持災金剛
奉請大神金剛 奉請安慰尼金剛
金剛般若波羅密經
如是我聞一時佛在舍衞國祇樹給孤獨園與大
比丘衆千二百五十人俱爾時世尊食時著衣持

（下段 陀羅尼）

薩婆悉唎 末麗 八
摩塞訖栗帝 南
地目帝 跋折羅
九
婆盧羯薩婆
薩婆薩埵 十
薩婆薩埵薩埵婆尼 十一
吽 引 羅擎聲 毗
伐嚼毗泥 十二
娑翻播波 引
薩婆橋波 引
燒達尼 娑
訶 引

佛々々
人の今代
毎々延は
海出入ろそ
之梅の神風
天弥彦

where the papyrus plant grew freely in the Nile valley, later of Rome and Byzantium. Firmus, the imperial Roman pretender in AD 273 boasted that he could keep a whole army on the revenues from the papyrus trade. There is some irony in the fact that the word 'paper', the name of the material which supplanted papyrus in the 11th century AD, is derived, via French and Latin, from the Greek 'papyros'.

Since the days of antiquity much has been written about the use, and even more about the production, of papyrus. Basically, carefully cut pieces from the inner stem of the plant were laid cross-wise (one layer on top of the other) on a special table, pressed or beaten together and then dried in the sun. Some type of adhesive was without doubt necessary but none of the classical or Arab writers is very clear on this point; suggestions ranged from the natural property of muddy Nile water to gum, starch or a special type of glue made in Egypt from flour, hot water and vinegar. Several sheets were stuck together, the best being placed at the beginning with those of inferior quality coming towards the end of each roll. Papyrus could be produced in a wide variety of different qualities: fine thin pale sheets on one hand and thick brown carton-like packing 'paper' on the other. Basically a brittle material, earthenware pots, glass containers and parchment envelopes were sometimes used for its protection, especially in the case of documents. With the beginning of the Christian era papyrus became increasingly scarce and in consequence more expensive, with the codex form, where both sides could be inscribed, taking precedence over the scroll format. In the hey-day of papyrus production large plantations flourished around manufacturing centres like Alexandria, Memphis and Sais. Nowadays the plant has almost disappeared from the Nile Valley. Outside Egypt it still grows in the Sudan, in Ethiopia and, most important, in Sicily near Syracuse where it was probably introduced during the Arab occupation and where it is still used, though on a very modest scale, for the production of writing material.

Finally we come to paper, another triumph of traditional technology. The place of origin is once more China; the person generally thought responsible for its invention Cai Lun, a minister at the court of the Han Emperor Wu Di; the date AD 105. Many factors led to the invention of paper, the ever growing cost of silk, the cumbersome nature of bamboo books and the already mentioned practice of re-using old silk rags for creating a thin, paper-like material. But even old silk rags were expensive and the patent which Cai Lun finally perfected replaced silk by macerated linen rags mixed with mulberry bark, fishnets and used sandals. Within a very short time the Chinese were able to make excellent paper, relying mainly on

12 *Papyrus*

Scribes were the Civil Servants of ancient Egypt who enjoyed considerable privileges and considered themselves superior to other men. Even high officials had themselves shown as scribes in their votive and funerary statuary. This sculpture comes from Thebes (25th dynasty *ca* 750 BC) and shows Pes-Shu-Per, Chamberlain of the Divine Votress of Amun, Amenirdis, squatting in the scribal pose. His kilt, stretched tight, acts as a support for the papyrus on which he is shown writing. Scribal equipment hangs from his left shoulder and an ink palette rests on his left thigh. (British Museum, Department of Egyptian Antiquities 1514).

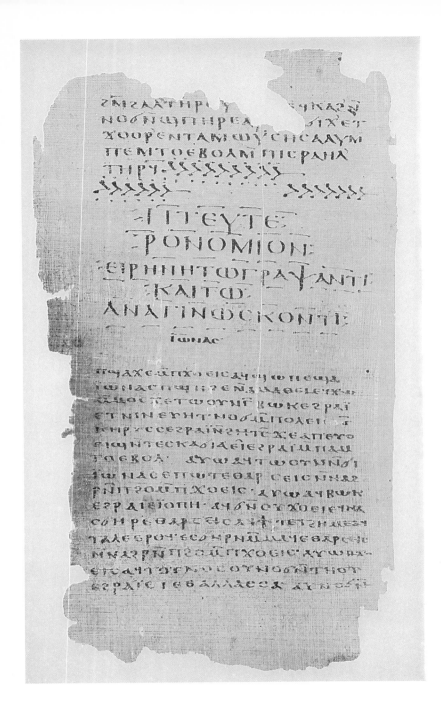

13 *Papyrus*

Folio from a Coptic Bible written in the Sa'idic dialect on papyrus showing the beginning of the Deuteronomy; from Upper Egypt; early 4th century AD. (Or. 7594. f. 53).

linen which was left to rot and then cleaned, bleached, pulped, bound with some suitable mixture like wheat flour and, finally, the resulting mixture spread on a frame to dry.

Paper reached Europe a thousand years after its invention in China, by a tortuous and not always easily traceable route. The manufacturing process had originally been a closely guarded state monopoly and during the first six hundred years the technique was known only in China from which it did not spread further west than Chinese Turkestan. In AD 751 the Muslim Governor of Samarkand, whilst repulsing a Chinese attack on the city, is reported to have taken 20,000 Chinese prisoners, some of them adept in the art of paper making. According to one version those men voluntarily set up paper-making shops in Samarkand but another version claims that they betrayed their secret only under torture. For the next hundred years Samarkand paper became as important an export article as Chinese paper but the social and religious structure of Islam is averse to localised exclusiveness and soon paper was made in the Middle East; Baghdad, Damascus, Tiberius, Hamah, Tripoli and later Cairo became manufacturing centres. The demand for raw material increased, and 'Abd al-Laṭīf, a doctor from Baghdad who stayed in Egypt between AD 1193 and 1207, reports how Egyptian peasants were robbing graves to obtain mummy wrappings made of linen, either for clothes, or to sell to paper factories. In the 12th century the Arabs introduced paper to Spain and Sicily, a century later to India. Rags remained the most important ingredient; in the laws of Alfonso X of Spain (AD 1236) paper is referred to, rather fittingly, as 'cloth parchment'. When, in AD 1492, the Muslims lost Spain the art of paper-making passed into the hands of less skilled Christian craftsmen and, almost immediately, the quality of paper declined. But in the following centuries paper established itself firmly in Europe. The manufacturing process remained basically the same until the 19th century when, once again for economic reasons (the spread of general education caused a sudden increase in demand), wood was introduced as a substitute for linen. The switch safeguarded quantity but it sacrificed quality. Paper as we know it today is in every way, in quality, durability and appearance, inferior to Oriental paper.

Rice-paper, incidentally, has little to do with paper or rice. It is made from the pith of a small tree (*Aralia papyrifera*) which grows mainly in the swampy forests of Formosa by a process similar to the one used for manufacturing papyrus.

Finally there are the truly unusual and extravagant materials used for very special occasions. Fruits: apples, lemons or peaches, inscribed with secret messages of love are mentioned in the Tales of Shahrazād and other contemporary sources. Henna was used for writing verses into the palms of slave girls, and secret messages were written with yogurt or onion juice on papyrus and made visible by covering the text, in the first case, with papyrus leaf ashes, in the second, by holding the sheet close to the fire.

WRITING IMPLEMENTS

Implements used for writing have their own history, a history which is unfortunately too long and too complex to be discussed here in detail. We have already seen that the actual process of writing can be executed in two distinctly different ways: the script can either be scratched into the surface of the material with a sharp instrument (stylus, knife, stone cutter's tool) or it can be applied on to the surface with a pen (quill, reed, wood or metal) or a brush, using ink, paint or lacquer. The process of transfer, when a rubbing is taken from a stone or metal inscription, represents an intermediate stage which, taken to its logical conclusion, leads to printing. It is certainly no accident that in many languages the word used for 'writing' is in some way derived from verbs meaning 'to paint', 'to cut', 'to incise' or 'to scratch'. Ink has been used since antiquity and a variety of recipes for its preparation has been handed down to us. Most of them have lamp black as a basic constituent combined, according to the desired effect, with resin, gum, honey, borax, in the case of coloured inks a colouring agent (sometimes gold or silver), burnt almonds or cows' urine.

Studying the history of human achievement in any given field, one is indeed inclined to agree with Goethe's Faust that true originality is almost impossible, that nearly everything has, if not been done before, at least been attempted. In the 10th century AD the Caliph al-Muʿizz expressed the wish for a pen capable of carrying its own supply of ink, where the ink would flow only when the pen was used for writing so that at other times it could safely be carried in his sleeve without fear of soiling his clothes. A clear specification for a fountain pen! What is more, the Caliph had his wish fulfilled: after some abortive attempts his craftsmen presented him with such a pen, made (naturally) in pure gold.

Diringer, D.: *The hand-produced book,* 3rd ed., London, 1952

Francis, F.: *Treasures of the British Museum,* London, 1971

Hedin, S. A.: *The Silk Road* (translated by F. H. Lyon), London, 1938

Jensen, H.: *Sign, Symbol and Script,* 2nd ed., London, 1970

Mitchell, T. C.: *Sumerian Art illustrated by Objects from Ur and Al-'Ubaid,* London, 1969

Oriental Manuscripts, London, 1973

Pattie, T. S. and Turner, E. G.: *The written Word on Papyrus,* London 1974

Safadi, Y. H.: *Islamic Calligraphy,* London, 1978

Vervliet, H. D. L.: *The Book through 5000 Years,* London, 1972

Wellard, J.: *By the waters of Babylon,* London, 1972

Writing in ancient Western Asia: its origins and development from pictures to letters, London, 1968